HABITAT SURVIVAL

GRASSLANDS

Buffy Silverman

Raintree

Chicago, Illinois

www.capstonepub.com
Visit our website to find out more information about Heinemann-Raintree books.

To order:
☎ Phone 800-747-4992
🖥 Visit www.capstonepub.com
to browse our catalog and order online.

© 2013 Raintree
an imprint of Capstone Global Library, LLC
Chicago, Illinois

Edited by Nancy Dickmann, Kristen Kowalkowski, and Claire Throp
Designed by Philippa Jenkins
Original illustrations © Capstone Global Library Ltd 2013
Illustrations by Oxford Designers and Illustrators, and Words and Publications
Picture research by Tracy Cummins
Originated by Capstone Global Library Ltd
Printed and bound in the United States of America, North Mankato, Minnesota.

18 17 16
10 9 8 7 6 5

Library of Congress Cataloging-in-Publication Data
Silverman, Buffy.
  Grasslands / Buffy Silverman.
    p. cm.—(Habitat survival)
  Includes bibliographical references and index.
  ISBN 978-1-4109-4596-9 (hb)—ISBN 978-1-4109-4605-8 (pb) 1. Grasslands—Juvenile literature. I. Title.
  QH87.7.S59 2013
  577.5'5—dc23   2012000234

082016
009949RP

Acknowledgments
We would like to thank the following for permission to reproduce photographs: Corbis pp. 18 (© Anthony Bannister/Gallo Images), 26 (© Jan Butchofsky), 29 (© Drew Myers); FLPA pp. 7, 10 (Ariadne Van Zandbergen), 8 (Neil Bowman), 11 (Jurgen & Christine Sohns), 14 (David Hosking), 21 (Tui De Roy), 27 (Nathan Lovas/Minden Pictures); Getty Images pp. 16 (EVARISTO SA/AFP), 23 (Antonio Scorza/AFP), 24 (Brooke Whatnall), 25 (Mike D. Kock); istockphoto pp. 4 (© Bruce Block); Nature Picture Library p. 13 (Gabriel Rojo); Shutterstock pp. 5 (© Rusty Dodson), 12 (© Sergey Timofeev), 15 (© agap), 22 (© My Portfolio); Superstock p. 17 (© Mauritius).

Cover photograph of a lion on the savanna in Africa reproduced with permission of Corbis/ © Chase Swift.

Every effort has been made to contact copyright holders of any material reproduced in this book. Any omissions will be rectified in subsequent printings if notice is given to the publisher.

Contents

Some words are shown in bold, **like this**. You can find out what they mean by looking in the glossary.

What Is a Grassland?

In a **prairie**, a black-tailed prairie dog nibbles on grass. A huge bison is also **grazing** on the prairie grass. Suddenly, the prairie dog hears an alarm call. Another prairie dog has spotted danger. A bald eagle is flying overhead, looking for food. The prairie dogs dive into a tunnel and wait until the eagle flies away.

Living on a grassland

The prairie dogs, bison, and bald eagle live in the same **habitat**. The habitat is called a grassland. Grasslands are often flat, open places that are mainly covered in tall grasses. Small flowering plants also grow there, but there are few trees.

Elephants live on grasslands.

Prairie dog town

Prairie dogs live together in large groups. They build huge underground tunnels. Each family lives in several rooms. There are chambers (rooms) for sleeping, storing food, and raising young. There are even separate chambers for going to the bathroom!

Grasslands provide habitats for many different animals. Birds, insects, and lizards find seeds to eat. **Mammals** graze on grasses. Other animals hunt the plant eaters. The animals and plants in a grassland depend on each other to survive.

On the Savanna

Tropical grasslands are called **savannas**. A savanna is warm all year. Heavy rains fall for about six months. Then little or no rain falls for months, and many fires occur. Without fire, many trees would grow and the savannas would turn into forests.

Savanna plants must be able to survive **drought** and fire. They have **adapted** to live with little water. Savanna grasses turn brown during the dry season, but their underground roots store food and **nutrients**. When rain falls, the grasses will grow again from the roots.

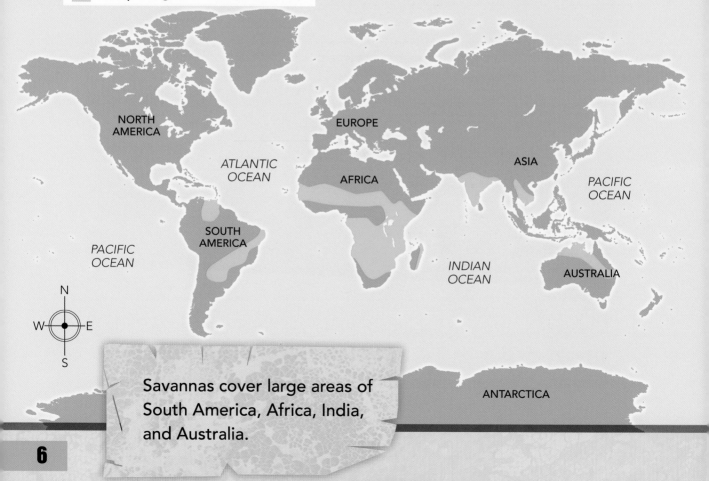

Tropical grasslands (savannas)

NORTH AMERICA

EUROPE

ATLANTIC OCEAN

AFRICA

ASIA

PACIFIC OCEAN

SOUTH AMERICA

PACIFIC OCEAN

INDIAN OCEAN

AUSTRALIA

N
W   E
S

ANTARCTICA

Savannas cover large areas of South America, Africa, India, and Australia.

These baobab trees are growing on an African savanna.

Savanna trees

Baobab trees grow on African and Australian savannas. They survive droughts by storing water inside their large trunks during the rainy season. They use the water during the dry season. The baobab trees also shed their leaves during a drought, which helps them to lose less water. Their thick bark helps them survive fires.

Savanna makers

Elephants can turn forests into savannas. They eat bark, smash branches, and knock over tree trunks. This makes space for grasses to grow.

Prairies and Steppes

Grasslands also grow in cooler places, called **temperate** regions. Here the winters are mild. Summers are warm, and fires sometimes burn. Trees and bushes grow along streams, where soil is wetter.

Prairies are one kind of temperate grassland. Many wildflowers bloom on prairies. Prairie plants die in winter, but their roots stay alive deep in the soil. When rain falls in spring and early summer, grasses grow back from the roots. They grow to be taller than a person.

Temperate grasslands

NORTH
AMERICA

EUROPE

ASIA

ATLANTIC
OCEAN

PACIFIC
OCEAN

AFRICA

PACIFIC
OCEAN

SOUTH
AMERICA

INDIAN
OCEAN

AUSTRALIA

N
W E
S

ANTARCTICA

South American **pampas**, South African velds, Russian steppes, and North American prairies are all grasslands.

This gerbil is eating a plant on an Asian steppe.

Hot and dry

Steppes are another type of temperate grassland. Summers on a steppe are hot and dry. Less rain falls than on a prairie, which means grasses do not grow as tall or as thick. Steppe grasses are **adapted** to survive in dry places. Their thin blades lose less water than plants with wide leaves.

Seed scatterer

Tumbleweed grows on Asian steppes and American prairies. When it is fully grown, a tumbleweed plant dries and breaks off from its roots. It forms a ball and tumbles in the wind, scattering seeds.

Living on a Savanna

Many of the animals on African **savannas**, such as zebras and wildebeests, eat the savanna grasses. Ostriches peck at seeds and roots. Giraffes reach to the treetops to eat acacia leaves. Other animals, such as cheetahs, hunt the plant eaters. The dry grass hides them as they hunt.

Herds of animals travel together on a savanna, searching for food and water.

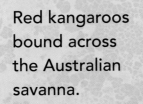

Red kangaroos bound across the Australian savanna.

Night flyers

Many of the animals on Australian savannas are active at night. Small bats find insects to eat. Larger bats, called flying foxes, drink sweet liquid called nectar, made by wildflowers. Flying foxes carry **pollen** from one flower to another as they feed. This helps savanna plants make seeds.

Termites are a type of insect that lives on savannas. They build tall mounds where large groups live and work together. The termites eat dead grass and trees. Their waste returns plant **nutrients** to the soil. That makes the soil better for growing plants. Termites also help plants by tunneling through soil. The tunnels allow water to trickle down into the soil.

Living on a Prairie

Many animals live on **prairies** and **steppes**. In summer, there is plenty of food, but in the winter it is harder to find.

Prairies are full of insects. Some of them, such as grasshoppers, eat grass. Others, such as butterflies, sip nectar from plants. Mole crickets dig underground tunnels where they lay eggs.

Corsac foxes hunt ground squirrels on steppes.

Grassland hunters

Tall prairie grasses hide predators while they hunt. A South American **pampas** cat stalks guinea pigs and mice in the tall grass. It also eats chicks and eggs of birds that nest in grasses.

Ground nesters

Many prairie birds eat seeds and insects. Grasshopper sparrows hunt grasshoppers and crickets. There are few trees for nesting, so they build their nests on the ground. Thick grasses help hide the nests from **predators**.

Small **mammals** such as mice and voles come out at night, when it is safer. They eat roots and seeds. They scurry along the ground and tunnel through tall grass. Sometimes they drop seeds, which grow into new plants.

Surviving Seasons

When seasons change, water and food may become harder to find. Heavy rains fall on the **savanna** in the wet season, helping plants grow. The savanna animals can find plenty to eat. After the rains stop, however, there is little food and water.

Some animals survive by **migrating**. Wildebeests, gazelles, and zebras follow rains to find grass in other places. Many birds also migrate. Other animals, such as giraffes, can live for a long time without water. When giraffes find water, they drink 10 gallons (38 liters) a day. Lizards hide underground so they lose less water. They hunt at night, and eat less during **droughts**.

During a drought, animals flock to shrinking water holes.

A bison's thick coat keeps it warm during winter.

Cold winds

Winter brings wind and snow to **steppes** and **prairies**. Bison use their heads like plows, pushing the snow away to find grass underneath. Many insects die in the winter. Before winter comes, they lay their eggs underground, and the eggs hatch in spring.

Finding water

Elephants have ways to find water all year round. They dig for water with their tusks. They tear open baobab tree trunks to find water.

Fire!

Fires are common on grasslands. They stop the grasslands from becoming forests. The roots of young trees are shallow, so they cannot grow back after a fire. Grasses burn, too, but their roots reach deep into the soil. They grow back, and they have more space with the trees gone.

Fires can start when lightning strikes. The wind spreads the fire, which burns dry grassland plants. Some animals, such as wild horses, run away from the fire. Others, such as snakes, survive underground. Only the top layer of soil heats up during a fire, so worms and insects crawl deep down to stay safe.

Animals flee from a grassland fire. They return after grasses grow back.

After a fire, grasses grow quickly and make seeds. Gouldian finches come and eat the grass seed.

Growing back

Savanna plants leave behind a layer of black ash after a fire. This adds **nutrients** to the soil and helps grasses to grow back when the rainy season comes.

Fire feast

Some animals find more food than usual after a fire. Birds eat grasshoppers, beetles, and lizards that were killed in the blaze. They also find mice that ran away from the fire.

Savanna Food Webs

Plants and animals on a **savanna** need each other to survive. All living things need **energy** to live and grow. They get energy from food. A food web shows how energy flows from one living thing to another. Trees, grasses, and plants make their own food. They use the Sun's energy to make food in their leaves.

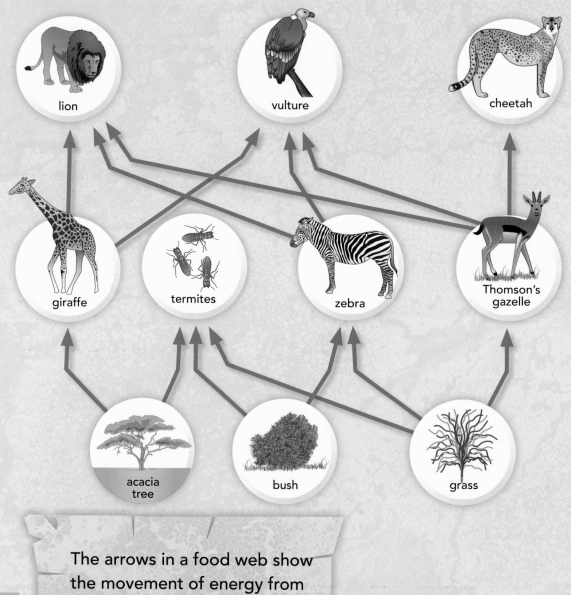

The arrows in a food web show the movement of energy from one living thing to another.

Long tongues

A giraffe's tongue is long and strong. It can reach around sharp thorns to pluck leaves. Giraffes may feed for 16 to 20 hours a day.

Plant eaters

Some animals get energy by eating plants. For example, zebras eat grasses, as well as leaves and stems from bushes. Thomson's gazelles eat the tender grasses that zebras leave behind.

Other animals are **predators**. Their energy comes from eating other animals. Cheetahs hunt animals such as gazelles. Lions hunt larger animals such as giraffes and zebras.

Some animals, such as vultures and termites, eat dead plants and animals. Tiny **bacteria** break down anything that is left, putting **nutrients** back into the soil.

These termites are eating dried grass. Bacteria in their guts break down tough plant material.

Pampas Food Webs

Pampas are grasslands in South America. Plants and animals in the pampas depend on each other. Like all food webs, a pampas food web starts with plants. Pampas plants, such as grasses and shrubs, use the Sun's **energy** to make food in their leaves and blades. They need energy to grow and make seeds.

Many animals eat the pampas plants. For example, pampas deer eat grasses, shrub leaves, and seeds. Maras, which are related to guinea pigs, also eat grasses and shrubs. Insects such as grasshoppers feed on grasses, too.

Energy flows from one living thing to another in the pampas.

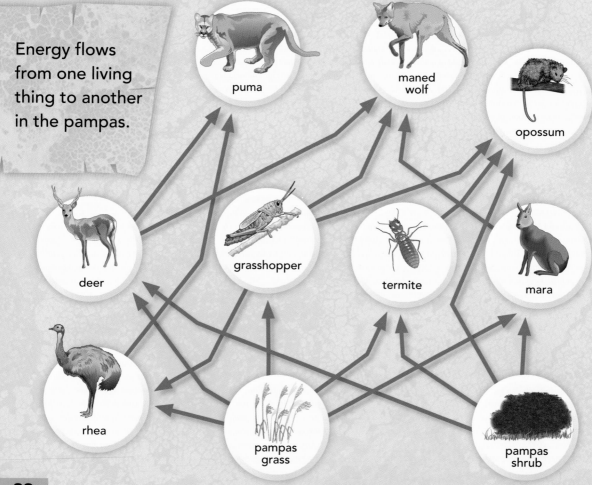

A maned wolf has long legs. This height helps it to see its prey above the tall grasses.

Running rheas

Rheas are large birds that cannot fly. Instead, they run across the grasslands. They swallow pebbles to help grind up tough plant food. Rheas also eat insects, lizards, frogs, small birds, and even snakes!

Omnivores

Animals that eat both plants and animals are called **omnivores**. White-eared opossums are omnivores. They eat seeds and fruits, as well as insects and small animals.

Some animals only eat other animals. Pumas stalk pampas deer and rheas. Maned wolves hunt maras, pampas deer, and insects at night.

Disappearing Grasslands

Grasslands cover about a quarter of Earth's land. Many of them have deep, rich soils. These soils are good for growing food, so farmers plow grasslands to plant corn and wheat. When this happens, grassland plants cannot grow.

People bring animals to **graze** on grasslands. They also build where wild grasses once grew. When people change grasslands, wild animals have a harder time finding food. There are fewer places for them to raise their young.

Farmers plant huge wheat fields on land where **steppe** grasses once grew.

Special savanna

The cerrado is the largest **savanna** in South America. It has more **native** plants and animals than any other savanna. In the past 50 years, people have changed the cerrado. Farms, roads, and buildings now cover much of it.

Stopping fire

People who live near grasslands fight wildfires to **protect** their homes. However, grasslands need regular fires to stay clear. When people prevent fires, trees grow and dead plants pile up. After many years without fire, huge fires can occur. These fires harm plants and animals, and damage people's homes.

Protecting Savannas

People have changed most of the world's **savannas**. However, people are working to **protect** the savannas that remain. When these **habitats** are protected, it helps the animals that live there.

Saving savannas

The world's largest savanna is in northern Australia. It is home to kangaroos, parrots, lizards, and hundreds of other animals. They face many threats, including cattle, bush fires, and **mining**. Many groups are joining together to protect this habitat. They are returning it to the way it was used in the past.

In some areas of Australia, the red-tailed black cockatoo is in danger of dying out.

New country, new chance

South Sudan is a new African country. It is home to many antelope, which **migrate** long distances to find food and water. Scientists have studied their routes. Now they are trying to get the government of South Sudan to protect these lands.

The African Wildlife Foundation

The African Wildlife Foundation works to protect Grevy's zebra. This zebra has lost much of its habitat to farms and cities. The zebras must compete with cattle for water and food. The foundation works with people who live near zebras. They learn to use land in ways that do not harm zebras.

Protecting Steppes and Prairies

The Mongolian **steppes** are the world's largest **temperate** grasslands. For thousands of years, Mongolian herders lived on steppes. They moved their sheep, goats, and cattle to find grass and water. Many Mongolian families still live as **nomads**, but **mining**, oil drilling, and building damage the steppes. People are trying to **protect** this **habitat**. Scientists study which lands are most important for wildlife and people. Governments pass laws to protect water and plan how land will be used in the future.

People and animals share the Mongolian steppes.

Regrowing prairies

Prairies once stretched across the middle of North America. Almost all of these prairies were turned into farms and towns. Many groups work to protect the remaining prairies. They also replace some of the lost prairies by planting **native** grasses and wildflowers and using fire carefully to keep out trees. Prairie animals are returning to these places.

Prairie chickens return

Prairie chickens were once common on Minnesota prairies. When the prairies were turned into farms, most of the birds disappeared. Today, some old farms have become grasslands again, and prairie chickens are moving back to them.

You Can Help Grasslands

Some grassland plants and animals need protection to survive. See if you can visit a grassland. There may be a meadow near your home. Learn about the plants and animals that live there, and share what you learn with your family. You might be able to volunteer for a group that **protects** grasslands, or join a group that watches birds in grasslands.

Be careful

You can also help protect grasslands that you visit. Clean your shoes before you go hiking. This ensures you are not carrying seeds that do not belong in the grassland you visit. Always stick to paths, and remember to take your trash away with you.

Saving grasslands

Grassland **habitats** are home to fascinating plants and animals. Many people around the world try to protect them. Where grasslands have disappeared, people work to replant them. Keeping grasslands safe means that plants and animals will have a place to live.

You can help protect your local meadow or grassland by picking up litter.

Glossary

adapt change in order to survive in a particular place

bacteria microscopic organisms that break down dead matter

drought long period of dry weather

energy power needed to grow, move, and live

graze eat grass and other green plants

habitat place where a plant or animal lives

herd wild animals that feed and travel together

mammal warm-blooded animal that usually has fur or hair and drinks milk from its mother when it is young

migrate move from one area to another

mining digging deep into the ground to search for substances such as coal, gemstones, and oil

native plant or animal that belongs in a certain place

nomad person who has no fixed home and moves from place to place to find food, water, and grazing land for his or her animals

nutrient chemical in food that helps things to grow

omnivore animal that eats plants and animals

pampas grassland of South America

pollen small grains that are male parts of a flower. Pollen combines with eggs to make seeds.

prairie grassland of North America

predator animal that hunts and eats other animals

prey animal that is hunted and eaten by another animal

protect keep from harm

savanna tropical grassland with trees scattered on it

steppe dry, temperate grassland

temperate area where temperatures are usually mild

tropical area on either side of the equator

Find Out More

Books

Jackson, Kay. *Explore the Grasslands* (Fact Finders). North Mankato, Minn.: Capstone, 2007.

Kalman, Bobbie. *Baby Animals in Savanna Habitats.* New York: Crabtree, 2011.

Pattison, Darcy. *Prairie Storms.* Mount Pleasant, S.C.: Sylvan Dell Publishing, 2011.

Rice, William. *African Grasslands* (Time For Kids Nonfiction Readers). Huntington Beach, Calif.: Teacher Created Materials, 2011.

Internet Sites

Facthound offers a safe, fun way to find Internet sites related to this book. All of the sites on Facthound have been researched by our staff.

Here's all you do:

Visit *www.facthound.com*

Type in this code: 9781410945969

Index